D1411051

BRACHIOSAURUS

LEIGH ROCKWOOD

PowerKiDS
press™
New York

Published in 2012 by The Rosen Publishing Group, Inc.
29 East 21st Street, New York, NY 10010

Copyright © 2012 by The Rosen Publishing Group, Inc.

All rights reserved. No part of this book may be reproduced in any form without permission in writing from the publisher, except by a reviewer.

First Edition

Editor: Joanne Randolph
Book Design: Kate Laczynski

Photo Credits: Cover, title page by Brian Garvey; cover background (palm tree leaves) © www.iStockphoto.com/dra_schwartz; cover background (palm tree trunk) iStockphoto/Thinkstock; cover background (ginkgo leaves) Hemera/Thinkstock; cover background (fern leaves) Brand X Pictures/Thinkstock; cover background (moss texture) © www.iStockphoto.com/Robert Linton; pp. 4–5, 11, 14, 16–17, 18, 20, 21 © 2011 Orpheus Books Ltd.; p. 6 Highlights for Children/Getty Images; p. 7 Colin Keates/Getty Images; p. 8 Shutterstock.com; pp. 9, 22 Louie Psihoyos/Getty Images; p. 10 © www.iStockphoto.com/Mogens Trolle; pp. 12, 13 DEA Picture Library/Getty Images; p. 15 De Agostini Picture Library/Getty Images; p. 19 Tony Waltham/Robert Harding/Getty Images.

Library of Congress Cataloging-in-Publication Data

Rockwood, Leigh.
  Brachiosaurus / by Leigh Rockwood. — 1st ed.
      p. cm. — (Dinosaurs ruled!)
  Includes index.
  ISBN 978-1-4488-4971-0 (library binding) — ISBN 978-1-4488-5092-1 (pbk.) — ISBN 978-1-4488-5093-8 (6-pack)
  1. Brachiosaurus—Juvenile literature. I. Title.
  QE862.S3R5553 2012
  567.912—dc22
                                     2011000098

Manufactured in the United States of America

CPSIA Compliance Information: Batch #WS11PK: For Further Information contact Rosen Publishing, New York, New York at 1-800-237-9932

CONTENTS

MEET THE BRACHIOSAURUS

The brachiosaurus was one of the tallest dinosaurs that ever lived. Most of that height came from its neck, which could be up to 30 feet (9 m) long! "Brachiosaurus" means "arm lizard." It got this name because its front legs are much longer than its back legs, and they look almost armlike.

This dinosaur has been **extinct** for millions of years. How do scientists know about them,

then? Brachiosaurus **fossils** give **paleontologists** clues about the dinosaur. These clues help paleontologists come up with theories, or ideas, about what life was like for the brachiosaurus.

The brachiosaurus was known for its large size, long neck, and long front legs. It also had an arch of bone on the top of its head.

THE LATE JURASSIC PERIOD

Dinosaurs lived for millions of years. They became extinct 65 million years ago. Paleontologists use a system called geologic time to organize the history of life on Earth. The brachiosaurus lived during the Late Jurassic period, which lasted from about 160 to 145 million years ago.

Here a brachiosaurus eats plants in a deciduous forest like those that were common during the Late Jurassic period.

DINO BITE

Earth's continents were once a giant landmass, called Pangaea. By the end of the Jurassic period, Pangaea had started to break apart.

This is part of a femur, or thigh bone, from a brachiosaurus. A brachiosaurus's femur would have been about the size of a full-grown person.

The brachiosaurus belonged to a group of large, long-necked dinosaurs called sauropods. Other sauropods that lived during the Jurassic period were the camarasaurus, the supersaurus, and the ultrasaurus. Like other sauropods, the brachiosaurus was a plant-eating dinosaur. With its long neck, it could reach leaves high in the trees.

WHERE DID THE BRACHIOSAURUS LIVE?

Sedimentary rocks are made up of layers of mud, sand, and stone that have been pressed together for millions of years. Fossils form in sedimentary rocks when dead plants or animals become trapped in these layers of sediment. This is known as fossilization.

Brachiosaurus bones have been found in places such as Dinosaur National Monument, shown here, which is in Utah and Colorado. The bones are found in layers of rock called the Morrison Formation.

Here paleontologists work to uncover a number of Jurassic period fossils found at Dinosaur National Monument.

Brachiosaurus fossils have been found in the western United States, southern Europe, and northern Africa. These places are far apart today. They were closer together, though, in the Jurassic period, when the continents were one landmass, called Pangaea. Today these places have very different **climates**. When the brachiosaurus lived, the climate of all these lands was warm and humid.

THE BRACHIOSAURUS'S BODY

A full-grown brachiosaurus could be 40 to 50 feet (12–15 m) tall, and 30 feet (9 m) of that height was its neck! From head to tail, a brachiosaurus could be 85 feet (26 m) long. A dinosaur of the brachiosaurus's size likely weighed around 50 tons (45 t). That is equal to the weight of five elephants!

DINO BITE

The giraffe is a modern animal that has long front legs and a long neck that lets it reach leaves on tall trees.

The brachiosaurus was huge, with a long neck that it used to reach leaves high in the trees. Do you see that its front shoulders are longer than its back ones here?

The brachiosaurus walked on four legs. Unlike most other four-legged dinosaurs, its front legs were longer than its back legs. This kind of build let the brachiosaurus hold its head up high rather than closer to the ground, like many other sauropods.

NOTABLE NECK

The brachiosaurus's 30-foot-(9 m) long neck was made up of 12 bones, called **vertebrae**. Paleontologists theorize that the brachiosaurus needed to have a strong heart to hold its head so high and far away from the rest of its body. If the heart could not keep blood flowing to a brachiosaurus's brain, the dinosaur would faint!

The brachiosaurus is the only dinosaur known to

A brachiosaurus's neck was nearly half the length of its body. Scientists guess that a brachiosaurus was about 85 feet (26 m) long.

Here you can see what scientists think the organs inside a brachiosaurus's body looked like. Can you see the huge heart on the left side of the cutaway?

have had longer front legs than back legs. Due to its size and build, it likely did not move as fast as some dinosaurs. Paleontologists think that it could reach speeds of 12 miles per hour (19 km/h), though.

SMALL HEAD AND BIG NOSTRILS

The brachiosaurus may have had a big body and a sizable neck, but it had a very small head compared to the rest of its body. It and the other sauropods were among the least intelligent dinosaurs.

The brachiosaurus had large nostrils on top of its head. Paleontologists once thought the brachiosaurus

Paleontologists think that a thin skin may have covered the brachiosaurus's nostrils, which let it make noises.

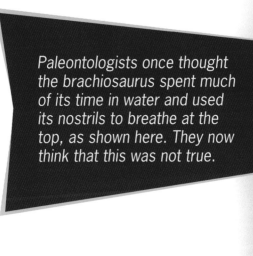

Paleontologists once thought the brachiosaurus spent much of its time in water and used its nostrils to breathe at the top, as shown here. They now think that this was not true.

spent much of its time underwater because of where its nostrils were. Today they think having the nostrils there may have helped it let heat out of its body. They also think these large nostrils meant that the dinosaur had a good sense of smell.

A Plant-Eating Dinosaur

The brachiosaurus was an **herbivore**. This meant it ate only plants. The brachiosaurus ate the leaves from trees such as conifers, cycads, and ginkgoes. It used its 52 chisel-like teeth to bite leaves, which it swallowed whole. It is thought that brachiosauruses also swallowed small stones, called **gastroliths**. Gastroliths helped break down the plant matter in the dinosaur's gut.

Brachiosauruses likely spent much of their day looking for and eating plants. Because they could reach high leaves, they did not have to compete with smaller animals for food, though.

Paleontologists guess that a dinosaur of the brachiosaurus's size would have needed to eat about 440 pounds (200 kg) of plant matter every day! Finding and eating that much would have been like a full-time job for the brachiosaurus.

DINO BITE

Some modern animals use small rocks to help them digest food. Birds swallow gravel to help them grind up food.

BRACHIOSAURUS HERDS

Paleontologists theorize that the brachiosaurus was a dinosaur that lived in small herds. There is safety in numbers since all the members of a herd can look out for **predators**.

Herds of brachiosauruses would have moved together to find new supplies of food. Young brachiosauruses would have walked in the center

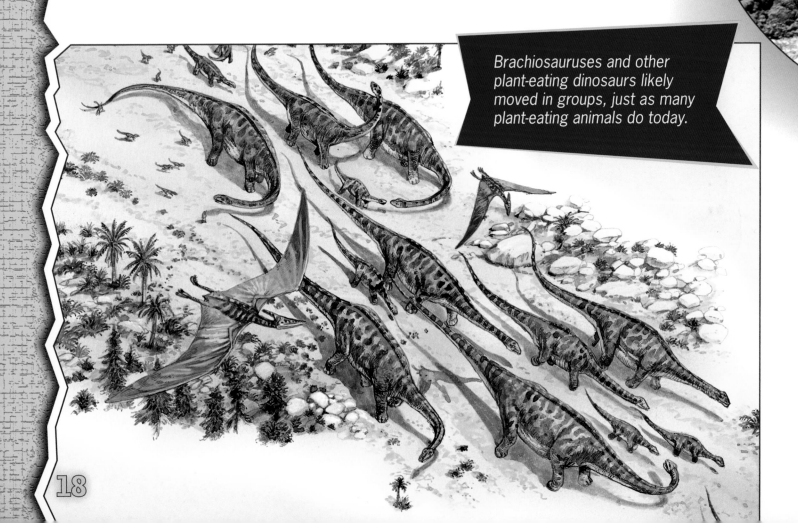

Brachiosauruses and other plant-eating dinosaurs likely moved in groups, just as many plant-eating animals do today.

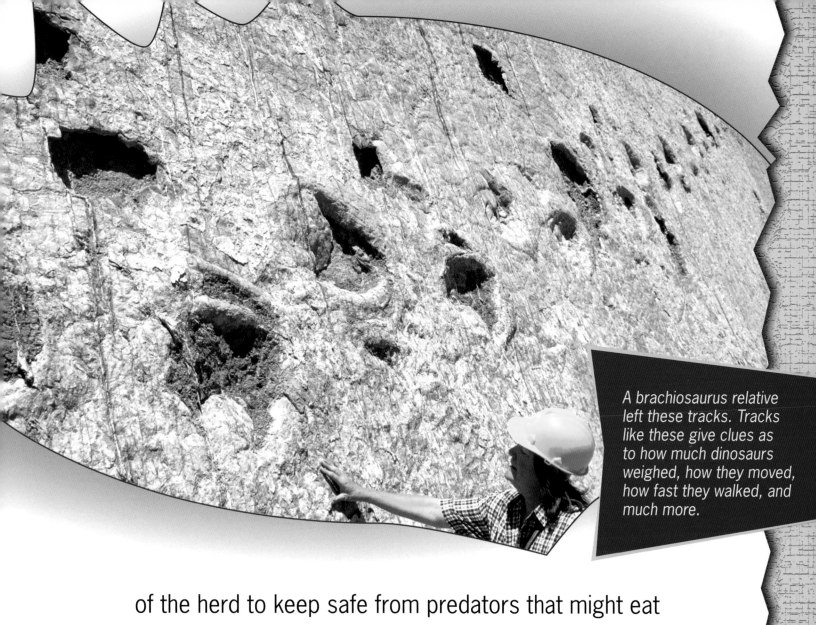

A brachiosaurus relative left these tracks. Tracks like these give clues as to how much dinosaurs weighed, how they moved, how fast they walked, and much more.

of the herd to keep safe from predators that might eat young dinosaurs, such as the allosaurus. Paleontologists came up with these theories of herd behavior from fossil clues. These clues include finding fossils of several of the same kind of dinosaur in one place and finding fossilized footprints that show many of the same kind of dinosaur moving in the same direction.

TOO BIG TO EAT?

A full-grown brachiosaurus was so big that paleontologists think that healthy adults had no predators. A meat eater like the allosaurus was half the brachiosaurus's size, making a brachiosaurus harder to kill than a smaller plant-eating dinosaur.

While the brachiosaurus's main **defense** was its size, it had other ways to **protect** itself. It could have

During the time brachiosauruses lived, there were lots of other dinosaurs around, too. It would have been easier for predators to catch and kill animals smaller than brachiosauruses.

used its tail to hit predators trying to take a bite. It also had sharp claws that could tear into enemies. A kick from a brachiosaurus would also have packed a punch!

Here you can see how big a brachiosaurus was compared with some of the predators of its time, such as the T. rex and spinosaurus. Some scientists think these meat eaters may have eaten young sauropods but generally did not bother with adults.

No Bones About It

The first brachiosaurus fossils were found in 1900, in Colorado. Paleontologist Elmer S. Riggs discovered and named the dinosaur.

Today paleontologists make **casts** of dinosaur fossils. Casts are both lighter and less fragile than fossilized bone. Paleontologists use

> Paleontologist Hermann Jaeger shows brachiosaurus bones that belong to the Humboldt Museum in Berlin, Germany.

computers and digital photographs of fossils from other dinosaurs of the same type to help them make casts of the bones missing from a skeleton. Computers also help them figure out how the dinosaur moved, so they can put the skeleton together the right way. One of the best-known brachiosaurus skeletons was once in Chicago's Field Museum. Today it stands tall in Chicago's O'Hare Airport.

GLOSSARY

casts (KASTS) Objects made by pouring something into a mold and letting it harden.

climates (KLY-mits) The kinds of weather certain places have.

defense (dih-FENTS) Something a living thing does that helps keep it safe.

extinct (ik-STINGKT) No longer existing.

fossils (FO-sulz) The hardened remains of dead animals or plants.

gastroliths (GAS-truh-liths) Stones swallowed by some animals to aid in the breakdown of food.

herbivore (ER-buh-vor) An animal that eats only plants.

paleontologists (pay-lee-on-TO-luh-jists) People who study things that lived in the past.

predators (PREH-duh-terz) Animals that kill other animals for food.

protect (pruh-TEKT) To keep safe.

sedimentary rocks (seh-deh-MEN-teh-ree ROKS) Stones, sand, or mud that has been pressed together to form rock.

vertebrae (VER-tuh-bray) Backbones, which protect the spinal cord.

INDEX

WEB SITES

Due to the changing nature of Internet links, PowerKids Press has developed an online list of Web sites related to the subject of this book. This site is updated regularly. Please use this link to access the list:
www.powerkidslinks.com/dinr/brach/